ideals® COUNTRY

MAY 2004

Dedicated to a celebration—through poetry and prose—of the American ideals of faith in God, loyalty to country, and love of family.

Summer's lease hath all too short a date.
—*William Shakespeare*

IDEALS—Vol. 61, No. 3 May 2004 IDEALS (ISSN 0019-137X, USPS 256-240) is published six times a year: January, March, May, July, September, and November by IDEALS PUBLICATIONS, a division of Guideposts, 39 Seminary Hill Road, Carmel, NY 10512. Copyright © 2003 by IDEALS PUBLICATIONS, a division of Guideposts. All rights reserved. The cover and entire contents of IDEALS are fully protected by copyright and must not be reproduced in any manner whatsoever. Title IDEALS registered U.S. Patent Office. Printed and bound in USA by Quebecor Printing. Printed on Weyerhaeuser Husky. The paper used in this publication meets the minimum requirements of American National Standard for Information Sciences—Permanence of Paper for Printed Library Materials, ANSI Z39.48-1984. Periodicals postage paid at Carmel, New York, and additional mailing offices. Canadian mailed under Publications Mail Agreement Number 40010140. POSTMASTER: Send address changes to Ideals, 39 Seminary Hill Road, Carmel, NY 10512. CANADA POST: Send address changes to Guideposts PO Box 1051, Fort Erie ON L2A 6C7. For subscription or customer service questions, contact Ideals Publications, a division of Guideposts, 39 Seminary Hill Road, Carmel, NY 10512. Fax 845-228-2115. Reader Preference Service: We occasionally make our mailing lists available to other companies whose products or services might interest you. If you prefer not to be included, please write to Ideals Customer Service.

ISBN 0-8249-1232-2 GST 893989236

Visit the *Ideals* website at www.idealsbooks.com

Cover: A lush wreath of sunflowers is draped over a primitive chair. Photograph by Linda and Alan Detrick/Grant Heilman.

Inside covers: Diane Phalen's HOLE IN THE BARN DOOR *portrays a lazy summer afternoon punctuated by the bright colors of comfortable quilts. Image provided by Diane Phalen Watercolors.*

In This Issue

Homesick

Cecil L. Gatten

Oh, for the land of the open sky
Where the eagle soars and hawk flies high,
Where grassy hills roll on and on,
And sky is a flame when day is gone.

There, rivers cut deep in the old flood plain,
And cedars grow on the rough terrain.
There creeks are clear as window glass,
And cattle roam through the knee-deep grass.

Give me the land of the open sky
When skeins of geese are flying by,
Where ducks make Vs in the meadow lakes,
And deer skip by in the canyon breaks.

There at night the skies are starred and still,
And coyotes howl from the highest hill.
All else is silence, still and deep.
It's easy to breathe and easy to sleep.

Youth

Emma Lazarus

Sweet, empty sky of June without a stain,
　　Faint, gray-blue mists on far-off hills,
Warm, yellow sunlight flooding mead and plain,
　　That each dark copse and hollow overfills;
　　The rippling laugh of unseen, rain-fed rills,
Weeds delicate-flowered, white and pink and gold,
A murmur and a singing manifold.

The gray, austere old earth renews her youth
　　With dew lines, sunshine, gossamer, and haze.
How still she lies and dreams, and veils the truth,
　　While all is fresh as in the early days!
　　What simple things be these the soul to raise
To bounding joy, and make young pulses beat,
With nameless pleasure finding life so sweet.

*Stanley Lake Creek reflects mountain peaks in the
wilderness of Sawtooth National Recreation Area,
Idaho. Photograph by Christopher Talbot Frank.*

ANOTHER PATH

Gladys Taber

Once I had a view from a real mountaintop in the Blue Ridge Mountains of Virginia. The sense of space was like a wind blowing from eternity. The farms below were Lilliputian checkerboards. Distant towns reminded me of a toy village I once had, with houses no bigger than thimbles. The lower ranges crested no more than a quiet surf over the green beaches of valleys. I felt no taller than a strawberry. At that moment, nothing mattered except the majesty of the mountaintop.

I can't always be on a peak, but I like to know it is there, offering serenity for the climbing.

I have need of the sky,
I have business with the grass;
I will up and get me away
*   where the hawk is wheeling*
Lone and high,
And the snow clouds go by.
I will get me away
*   to the waters that glass*
The clouds as they pass.
I will get me away to the woods.
I have need of the sky.
                    —RICHARD HOVEY

Paper birch trees frame a view of the White Mountains and Franconia Notch in Campton, New Hampshire. Photograph by William H. Johnson.

A Scherzo

Dora Greenwell

With the wasp at the innermost heart of a peach,
On a sunny wall out of tiptoe reach,
With the trout in the darkest summer pool,
With the fern seed clinging behind its cool
Smooth frond, in the chink of an aged tree,
In the woodbine's horn with the drunken bee,
With the mouse in its nest in a furrow old;
With the chrysalis wrapped in its gauzy fold;
With things that are hidden and safe and bold,
With things that are timid and shy and free,
Wishing to be;
With the nut in its shell, with the seed in its pod,
With the corn as it sprouts in the kindly clod,
Far down where the secret of beauty shows
In the bulb of the tulip, before it blows;
With things that are rooted and firm and deep,
Quiet to lie and dreamless to sleep;
With things that are chainless and tameless and proud.
With the fire in the jagged thundercloud,
With the wind in its sleep, with the wind in its waking,
With the drops that go to the rainbow's making,
Wishing to be with the light leaves shaking,
Or stones on some desolate highway breaking;
Far up on the hills, where no foot surprises
The dew as it falls or the dust as it rises;
To be couched with the beast in its torrid lair
Or drifting on ice with the polar bear,
With the weaver at work at his quiet loom;
Anywhere, anywhere, out of this room!

*A young woman daydreams by the ocean in this
contemporary painting by Guerennadi (Gennadi) Bernadsky
entitled* WATCHING THE WAVES. *Image from Fine Art
Photographic Library Ltd., London/Bourne Gallery
Reigate/Art Gallery Gerard, Wassenaar, Netherlands.*

At Home in My Tree

Debbie Craven

The elm tree by the barn is mine.
God made it just for me,
So I can imagine when I climb
That my home is in my tree.

From the fence I grab the first limb
To swing myself up high
And settle in my favorite seat
Where the branches make a Y.

I can see the pear trees down the path,
The wheat bent in the breeze.
But the leaves in my tree cuddle close;
I am hidden in walls of green.

I lean against the tree trunk,
A book upon my knees;
My lunch hangs from the branch above—
Home, sweet home, here in my tree.

Midsummer's Green

Jean A. Davidson

Fill your soul, your memory,
With layers and depths and textures
And heights of lush green,
Before the miracle of summer
Fades away once more, as it always does.

Drink in, absorb every hue and
Shade of green, from pale of mint
To the rich, dark splendor of evergreen forests.
Gaze at fields stretching far,
Like patchwork quilts of emerald,
Their edges stitched by fence-post embroidery.

Watch windswept grass swell like
Waves on a stormy sea, rippling
Over hills and valleys to wash upon

The rocky shores of stone walls.
Walk down peaceful wooded lanes,
Where ferns grow in lime-green flocks.

Listen with noise-weary ears to whispering
Leaves that speak of deep caverns
Of coolness and secret sun-dappled glades,
Sparkling with shifting chartreuse.

Sink into the shag carpet of deep-green moss.
Let your eyes dance along
With the softly swaying skirts
Of weeping willow's waltz.

Pines beckon with outstretched arms,
"Come, rest under my branches
On blankets of spice-scented summer."

Round hay bales are scattered across an open hillside in Osage County, Missouri. Photograph by Terry Donnelly.

Overleaf: Pink monkey flower, lupine, and other flowers bloom along the flowing waters of the Paradise River in Mount Rainier National Park, Washington. Photograph by Mary Liz Austin.

Lansing Christman

JUNE AFTERNOON

Today is one of those quiet days in June. It is still, the kind of day I like when summer comes to our hills and valleys. It is the time when the freshness of the morning dew quickly gives way to the heat of the afternoon, when thundershowers are welcome, and willows sway with the eddies of ducks. Even the flowers boast of their brightest apparel. The geraniums shout their reds, deep purple petunias raise their multiple faces, and day lilies trumpet all the variations of their golds and oranges and yellows. Cattails wave their wands in the slow breezes, and the visiting geese make the area lakes seem crowded.

June is a friendly month and kind. Earthy smells of fresh produce are the backdrop for cheery discussions at the farmers' market on the nurturing of small gardens. Neighbors share their bounty, particularly extra zucchini.

There is no wind to stir the grass and leaves. There are no blustery gales to sweep the timothy into those rhythmic undulations across the meadows. Only my footsteps bring a slight tremble to the grass as I walk slowly along.

Few songs float in the air now; the birds are nesting. Yet I do hear the call of the meadowlark and the field sparrow's song. I watch the bobolinks dip and dive over the fields. But down in the valley I know the barn swallows are sweeping in and out of the barns, where they have plastered their nests to beams and rafters and the hayfork "trolley" track. True pioneers of the sky, the hawks make their wide circles high, seemingly content today to just make the field mice scurry hurriedly under the barn and the timid rabbit stay still under the rosebushes.

I see the orange tabby, a recent visitor, and the elderly calico snoozing in the shade of an old maple tree. A long-eared hound has detoured down the road, oblivious to the cats, searching at an easy pace for something to startle with a bark.

In the meadows and fields I find a world of life around me, whose pulse resonates with mine, instilling in me an appreciation for the glory and wonder of each season in the outdoor world.

It is here, in the solitude of the country, that I find my summit of contentment in June's kind and gentle ways.

The author of four books, Lansing Christman has contributed to Ideals *for more than thirty years. Mr. Christman has also been published in several American, international, and braille anthologies. He lives in rural South Carolina.*

Vivid flowers offer their faces to the warm sun. Photograph by Steve Terrill.

READERS' REFLECTIONS

Readers are invited to submit original poetry for possible publication in future issues of IDEALS. *Please send typed copies only; manuscripts will not be returned. Writers receive payment for each published submission. Send material to Readers' Reflections, Ideals Publications, 535 Metroplex Drive, Suite 250, Nashville, Tennessee 37211.*

Solitude

Dolores Eggener
Marinette, Wisconsin

To walk alone on a summer eve,
To think—and then eventually leave
The cares of the day behind.
To lose one's self and now to find
In every step such joys!
To feel the balmy, tepid air
Blow softly on my cheeks and hair.
To hear the frogs and crickets sing
And watch the birds at day's end wing
Their way to swaying trees.
To watch in awe as clouds and sky
Explode with color and intensify,
Mirroring visions of setting sun,
Assurance that a day is done.
I pause in silent reverence.

View from the Road

Linda Schafer
Centerville, Ohio

Rising, turning left, then right,
Twisting, road fades out of sight.
Near side rises to the sky,
Cliffs so steep and trees so high.
Far side plunges down and down,
Gorge below bright orange and brown.
One more bend then brings a view,
Colors now of every hue.
Each direction gives a chance
To delight in nature's dance.
Through the hills and valleys deep,
I gather memories I can keep.

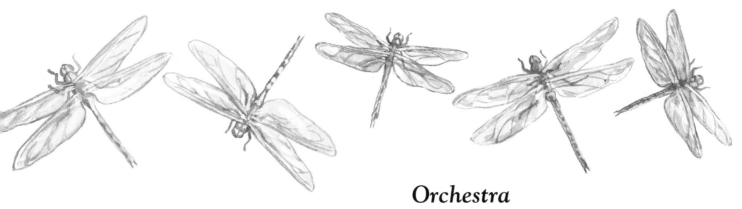

Orchestra
Karen A. Baughan
Luray, Virginia

The bees and the cicadas so perfectly express
The symphonies of summer heat that on these mornings press,
And thunder rolls with apathy across the hazy hills,
Like timpani played largo time so all ambition stills.
And oak trees and cattle in breathless torpor stand,
While grass and flower, pond and puddle sink into the land;
Now a meadowlark sings descant above the rasping hum,
And eyes blink and locusts pause, then harmonize their thrum,
Till from His band the Maestro's hand releases evening showers.

Busy Days
Margaret F. Sharpless
Santa Rosa, California

Down by the haystack
Behind the barn,
Underneath the chicken coop
On the old country farm.
Up in the apple tree,
Down by the creek,
Up the path into the woods,
Playing hide and seek.
Into the buggy,
Laying down flat,
Underneath the Model T—
"Move over, old cat."
Into the house
All covered with mud,
Into the bath in a galvanized tub.
Up to the table to a wonderful surprise—
Chicken and dumplings
And homemade apple pies.
Up the creaky old stairs
And into my featherbed.
Old Sandman's coming;
What a busy day I've had.

Prelude to Summer Storm
Ruth M. W. Warren
Holiday, Florida

Filling the blue dome of the sky,
Mountainous billows of clouds rise
In white and gray.
Birds chirp tuneless songs of expectation.
Sudden flashes of lightning cross space
In bright display,
And thunder rumbles loudly in response
That a summer storm is passing
By this way.
Trees lift branches with thirsting leaves
And dry fields cry silently,
"Celebrate this day!"

15

Communication

Jennie M. Palen

Whether resenting the personal insult of rain,
upstaging her perennial enemy, the dog,
or cuffing the nonsense out of an explosion of kittens,
my unflappable cat
speaks more eloquently than many
an over-diploma'd diplomat.

Vignette of Summer

Frances Minturn Howard

On the cool thick grass under a sycamore
Is poured Mr. Jingle, the cat, a pool of blackness
So strong he seems to suck all shadow in,
Himself the essence of surrounding shade.
Egypt is in the crook of his straight tail.
The small carved bony triangle of face
Drawn out in Nubian profile, immobile
As any Pharaoh's. I'll not try
To guess his dreams, except he breathes out bliss
In sweet and regular cadence, sleep distilled,
To delicately steam the air above him,
Mingling with breath of wild white roses, clover,
Bay, gorse, wild broom. The leaf-bruised air of summer
Is honey-thick above his slumbering head,
While close beside a shaft of sun on grass
Gives him a hump of emerald on his back.
The scene is struck like a new-minted coin
Upon the mind; of many such small hoards
Whole seasons reconstruct; joy's random gold
Built up of such inconsequential scenes,
Oddly and inappropriately to bring, in cold
And sodden seasons, the scent of wild white rose,
And in a closed and sunless winter room
Summer's spreading green stain.

A tabby cat chooses to pose near flowering geraniums. Photograph by Daniel Dempster.

THE OLD WOODSHED

Norma Sworski

I like to think of our old woodshed,
With its crooked, sagging door,
Where the logs, chopped for the winter,
Lie in heaps upon the floor.

Bark and sawdust for a carpet,
Splinters often found bare toes.
And the switch above the doorway
We used to dust our clothes.

Outside walls showed carved initials
Left by generations past,

Linking hearts in love together,
Sworn throughout the years to last,
Giving to this ancient storehouse,
Leaning slightly to one side,
A stout determination,
Quiet dignity, and pride.

As a tree bent in a windstorm,
Scarred and weathered, yet it stood,
And in my private, happy thoughts still holds
Memories that are warm and good.

THE AUCTION SALE

Lela Hudson Decker

Did you ever see an auction
    Like the country people know,
Where they sell farm machinery
    And let some odd things go?

When a goodly crowd has gathered,
    Looked around at this and that,
Then the auctioneer gets ready,
    Adjusting his collar and hat.

The jargon that he uses
    Is so much Greek to me;
I hardly understand him,
    I just stand still and see:

There's a blue bowl and pitcher,
    But they're chipped, I do believe;

And the tiny cups and saucers—
    A young girl's set for tea?

The ladies from the town church
    Have a stand where folks can eat
Homemade pie and cake with coffee,
    Surely a delicious treat.

Now to farmer's plow and hay rake,
    To the tractors in the barn;
Livestock, too, is "Going, going,"
    "Two times, thrice" and now is "Gone."

It's been a day for dreaming,
    For meeting one more time
With friends to exchange banter
    To the auctioneering rhyme.

*Roses cascade over an abandoned
shed near Fort Bragg, California.
Photograph by Carr Clifton.*

TRAVELER'S DIARY

D. Fran Morley

KUTZTOWN FESTIVAL
KUTZTOWN, PENNSYLVANIA

In my mind, the long, lazy summer days of childhood flow seamlessly one to another, with little to distinguish a day in June from one in July or August. But one week every summer, the week of the annual county fair, stands out as a festival of sight, sound, and taste. At the time, our little fair was plenty big enough to impress and entertain my friends and me. We ate our fill of homemade goodies and roasted corn, chased baby pigs around a pen, tossed rings around bottles to win stuffed bears, and rode around and around on the carousel.

Such simple pleasures can be hard to find today, as they are often eclipsed by entertainment perceived to be "bigger and better." However, I was happy to discover that old-fashioned fun is the main attraction at a festival that has been held in tiny Kutztown, Pennsylvania, around the last week of June every year since 1950. After doing some preliminary research, I dug out my well-worn travel maps and quickly made plans to attend this year's event.

The Kutztown Festival honors the area's Pennsylvania Dutch heritage. Visitors from all over the world come to wander through the festival grounds and enjoy the traditional food and crafts, plus entertainment and seminars on rural life. Like most of the other visitors, I hope also to do some serious shopping.

There are over two hundred craftspeople selling their wares and demonstrating time-honored skills such as blacksmithing, spinning and weaving, chair caning, tole painting, broom making, and decoy carving. A big attraction is the annual quilt show and sale; this year, more than two thousand quilts, most made locally by Amish and Mennonite women, will be on display. I plan to be there for the excitement when the top twenty-four quilts go up for auction.

A young candlemaker cautiously dips wicks. Photograph courtesy of the Kutztown Festival.

The purpose of the festival has always been two-fold. It is designed to entertain all ages, but subtle lessons about the traditional Pennsylvania Dutch life are behind every game and activity. Children enjoy the old-time games, sing-alongs, hands-on craft projects, and folktales. I read that they line up to run through the giant hay maze and ride on an authentic nineteenth-century horse-drawn carousel. How enjoyable it must be for the grownups to see children having fun without the benefit of electronics!

Delicious food is available for festival-goers. Photograph courtesy of the Kutztown Festival.

I always appreciate home-cooked foods and farm-fresh produce, so on my visit I plan to spend time at the farmer's market section, where, I have learned, visitors may purchase cheese, Pennsylvania Dutch sausages and other meats, preserves, and even bread that has been baked on-site in a wood-burning oven. It will be difficult to resist snacking on my purchases, but I will want to save room for all the other delicious traditional foods that are served at the festival, including the popular family-style supper.

If I can draw myself away from the food and crafts, I hope to take in a few of the seminars that cover such topics as traditional herbal cures, covered bridges, and barn raisings. I have already learned that the term "Pennsylvania Dutch" derives from the word *Deutsche*, meaning

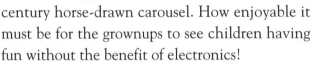
The Kutztown Festival honors the area's Pennsylvania Dutch heritage.

German, so the people we commonly call Pennsylvania Dutch are actually Pennsylvania Germans. I look forward to learning more about these fascinating people and their heritage.

It has been said that you can never recapture the days of your youth, and that's probably true. But I believe that the Kutztown Festival may be one of the best places to visit the past and enjoy a little taste of life from days gone by.

One of the many artists at the festival demonstrates his craft. Photograph courtesy of the Kutztown Festival.

When Fran Morley is not gallivanting around the country with her husband, Tom, they reside in Fairhope, Alabama, with their sixteen-year-old cat, Gracie.

SCARBOROUGH FAIR
Author Unknown

Where are you going? To Scarborough Fair?
Parsley, sage, rosemary, and thyme,
Remember me to a bonny lass there,
For once she was a true lover of mine.

Tell her to make me a cambric shirt,
Parsley, sage, rosemary, and thyme,
Without any needle or thread work'd in it,
And she shall be a true lover of mine.

Tell her to wash it in yonder well,
Parsley sage, rosemary, and thyme,
Where water ne'er sprung nor a drop of rain fell,
And she shall be a true lover of mine.

Tell her to plow me an acre of land,
Parsley, sage, rosemary, and thyme,
Between the sea and the salt sea strand,
And she shall be a true lover of mine.

Tell her to plow it with one ram's horn,
Parsley, sage, rosemary, and thyme,
And sow it all over with one peppercorn,
And she shall be a true lover of mine.

Tell her to reap it with a sickle of leather,
Parsley, sage, rosemary, and thyme,
And tie it all up with a tomtit's feather,
And she shall be a true lover of mine.

Tell her to gather it all in a sack,
Parsley, sage, rosemary, and thyme,
And carry it home on a butterfly's back,
And then she shall be a true lover of mine.

THROUGH MY WINDOW

Pamela Kennedy

FAIR DAY

Last summer a friend invited me to go to the state fair in Honolulu. We drove to the Aloha Stadium, parked, and walked to the fairgrounds, part of the blacktop parking lot, bounded by portable metal fencing. After paying our admission, we strolled among booths set up to sell popcorn, cotton candy, and local items like shaved ice, musubi and lau lau (chunks of meat or vegetables, steamed in ti leaves). Fairgoers crowded midway rides and game booths. Screams from the tilt-a-whirl blended with the cries of hawkers.

"Where are the pigs?" I asked.

"What pigs?" my friend responded.

"You know, the pigs, the cows, the rabbits, livestock exhibits. And what about the prize pumpkins?" I responded. "And when does the pie judging start?"

My companion looked at me and shook her head. "None of that here. Just rides and food and games. Oh, I think there's a guy who wrestles an alligator—'Kachunga, the American bushman'."

We left after an hour, without seeing Kachunga or his alligator. I wish I could have shown my friend a real "fair day," the kind of day that leaves you breathless with wonder. The kind I remember from my childhood.

Each year, on the third Friday in September, school would be canceled and we would all get free tickets to attend the Western Washington State Fair in Puyallup. The Puyallup Fair was a kaleidoscope for the senses. There were hot, buttery scones slathered with red raspberry jam, saltwater taffy still warm from the puller, caramel apples, vanilla ice-cream bars dipped in chocolate, and hamburgers piled high with savory golden onions. Scents and sounds and sights clamored for attention.

Dozens of wooden buildings held treasures waiting to be discovered. The Grange halls burst with fall's abundance. There were scenes of flying geese, or subtly colored landscapes created entirely of painstakingly placed produce, seeds, and eggs. Immense, lopsided pumpkins rested on wooden pallets waiting to be glorified as "best in show." The fruit of hands and hearts, quilts, handmade garments, cakes, jams, and pies lined walls and shelves. Multicolored dahlias and gladiolas crowded for attention, every bloom and bud carefully placed to catch the judge's eye.

But there was much more of life to experience beyond the exhibit halls. In pungent barns, I walked between rows of stomping cattle and watched a gentle Guernsey give up her cream to a hissing milking machine. Stacks of hutches housed rabbits of all kinds and colors. Sometimes, if I was very gentle, I could poke my finger through the wires and bury it deep in the warm, soft fur, feeling the rapid beating of the rabbit's heart. Hens and

A Special Invitation

TO SAVE UP TO 50% OFF THE COVER PRICE!

TERM	RETAIL VALUE	YOUR PRICE	YOU SAVE
1 year	$35.70	**$19.95**	$15.75
2 years	$71.40	**$35.95**	$35.45

My Name _____

Address _____

City _____

State _____ ZIP _____

☐ Start or Renew my own subscription   ☐ Payment enclosed

☐ 1 year   ☐ 2 years   ☐ Bill me later

Yes! SEND A GIFT SUBSCRIPTION AND GIFT ANNOUNCEMENT IN MY NAME TO:

Name _____

Address _____

City _____

State _____ ZIP _____

ideals®

Your first issue will arrive in 4 to 6 weeks.
Foreign and Canadian subscriptions: add $10 per
year, payable in U.S. funds. Limited offer. All
orders subject to approval.

05-20221123

BUSINESS REPLY MAIL

FIRST-CLASS MAIL   PERMIT NO. 38   CARMEL, NY

POSTAGE WILL BE PAID BY ADDRESSEE

IDEALS PUBLICATIONS
A DIVISION OF GUIDEPOSTS
PO BOX 795
CARMEL NY 10512-9904

NO POSTAGE
NECESSARY
IF MAILED
IN THE
UNITED STATES

roosters in the huge chicken coops raised a ruckus with their cackles and crows, drowning all conversation. But over in the corner, under the warm lights of an incubator, I could watch the miracle of birth as a tiny, wet chick fought its way out of an eggshell and lay, weak and panting, as its down dried.

In the "Pig Palace" carefully tended swine waited their turns at auction, while yearlings dashed around a small track sporting racing silks. And every year, there were at least of couple of huge sows with litters of piglets. The little Yorkshires grunted and pushed their way to their mothers' bellies. Lined up like plump pink sausages, they suckled greedily then napped on their oblivious brothers and sisters. Goats bleated and calves bawled and horses stomped their hooves at will. It was life and death and everything in between at the Puyallup fair.

When the setting sun tinted the air with gold, it was time to move to the midway. During the day, the midway was tacky and dusty, scarred by peeling paint and rusty metal. But after dark, traced with thousands of colored lights, it became a magical place. The roller coaster, carousel, and other rides swept me into a dark land of danger and excitement. I could scream in terror or laugh with hilarity. Everybody did and nobody cared.

I always finished up crammed full of caramel apples, sticky, tired, and wonderfully happy. And when, at the end of the day, my par-

A prancing horse awaits a rider in the Carousel Museum in Old Mystic, Connecticut. Photograph by R. Krubner/H. Armstrong Roberts.

ents drove me home, I kneeled on the seat for a last glimpse through the back window of our 1955 Plymouth. I didn't want to miss one single moment of Fair Day.

Pamela Kennedy is a freelance writer of short stories, articles, essays, and children's books. Wife of a retired naval officer and mother of three children, she has made her home on both U.S. coasts and currently resides in Honolulu, Hawaii.

Family Recipes

Cool, homemade ice cream on a hot, midsummer day is a taste treasure. And fruit and vegetables fresh from the garden are the blessings of summer food preparation. We would love to try your favorite recipe too. Send a typed copy to Ideals Publications, 535 Metroplex Drive, Suite 250, Nashville, Tennessee 37211. Payment will be provided for each recipe published.

Egg Salad

Betty J. Bunn, Donaldson, Arkansas

6 hard-boiled eggs, chopped
½ cup diced celery
2 tablespoons diced green pepper
1 teaspoon minced onion
2 tablespoons mayonnaise
1 tablespoon cider vinegar
1 tablespoon Worcestershire sauce
   salt and pepper to taste

In a medium mixing bowl, combine eggs, celery, green pepper, and onion. In a small bowl, combine remaining ingredients and mix well. Stir into egg mixture. Refrigerate, covered. Serve in scoops on lettuce leaves or crackers. Makes 6 servings.

Italian Beet Salad

Amelia Brumm, East Lansing, Michigan

3 14.5-ounce cans sliced beets, well drained
1 medium onion, thinly sliced
2 tablespoons chopped parsley
½ tablespoon oregano
2 teaspoons garlic salt
1 teaspoon cinnamon
⅓ cup olive oil
⅓ cup white vinegar
⅓ cup tarragon vinegar
¾ cup granulated sugar
1 teaspoon salt
   hard-boiled eggs, sliced, optional

In a large bowl, combine beets, onion, parsley, oregano, garlic salt, and cinnamon. Set aside. In a medium bowl, whisk olive oil and vinegars together; add sugar and salt and whisk until combined. Pour over beet mixture and refrigerate overnight. Garnish with slices of hard-boiled eggs. Makes 8 servings.

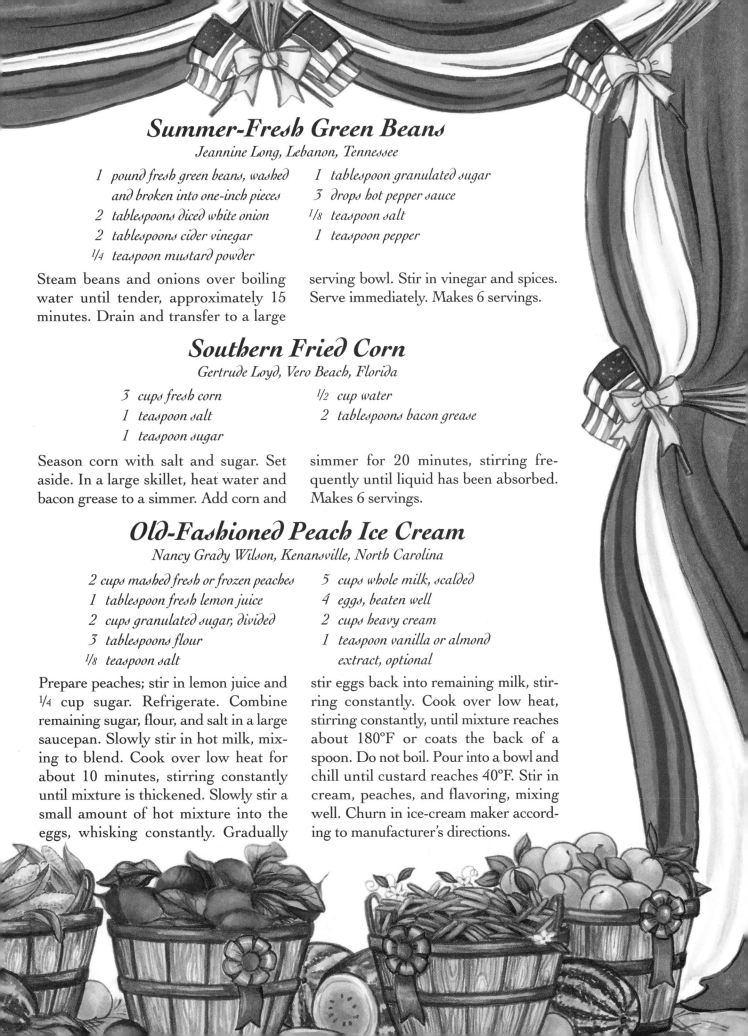

Summer-Fresh Green Beans

Jeannine Long, Lebanon, Tennessee

1 pound fresh green beans, washed and broken into one-inch pieces
2 tablespoons diced white onion
2 tablespoons cider vinegar
1/4 teaspoon mustard powder
1 tablespoon granulated sugar
3 drops hot pepper sauce
1/8 teaspoon salt
1 teaspoon pepper

Steam beans and onions over boiling water until tender, approximately 15 minutes. Drain and transfer to a large serving bowl. Stir in vinegar and spices. Serve immediately. Makes 6 servings.

Southern Fried Corn

Gertrude Loyd, Vero Beach, Florida

3 cups fresh corn
1 teaspoon salt
1 teaspoon sugar
1/2 cup water
2 tablespoons bacon grease

Season corn with salt and sugar. Set aside. In a large skillet, heat water and bacon grease to a simmer. Add corn and simmer for 20 minutes, stirring frequently until liquid has been absorbed. Makes 6 servings.

Old-Fashioned Peach Ice Cream

Nancy Grady Wilson, Kenansville, North Carolina

2 cups mashed fresh or frozen peaches
1 tablespoon fresh lemon juice
2 cups granulated sugar, divided
3 tablespoons flour
1/8 teaspoon salt
5 cups whole milk, scalded
4 eggs, beaten well
2 cups heavy cream
1 teaspoon vanilla or almond extract, optional

Prepare peaches; stir in lemon juice and 1/4 cup sugar. Refrigerate. Combine remaining sugar, flour, and salt in a large saucepan. Slowly stir in hot milk, mixing to blend. Cook over low heat for about 10 minutes, stirring constantly until mixture is thickened. Slowly stir a small amount of hot mixture into the eggs, whisking constantly. Gradually stir eggs back into remaining milk, stirring constantly. Cook over low heat, stirring constantly, until mixture reaches about 180°F or coats the back of a spoon. Do not boil. Pour into a bowl and chill until custard reaches 40°F. Stir in cream, peaches, and flavoring, mixing well. Churn in ice-cream maker according to manufacturer's directions.

COLLECTOR'S CORNER

Maud Dawson

FIESTA DINNERWARE

"Where did you get those beatiful red plates?" a friend of mine recently asked, as we were sitting at my kitchen table comparing notes on an upcoming birthday party. Her question about the bright red plates in my hutch reminded me of the family dinners of my childhood. The meals served in my parents' kitchen influenced my preference for red that has lasted many years. Dinner was a mandatory sit-down meal when I was a preteen. Each member of the family had to be present, and no one was served until my father was seated. The conversation was always lively. My brother announced his engagement during one dinner, and I reported my first grade of A on an English paper, among other noteworthy family news. Because of those pleasant memories associated with using the red dinnerware, I have always adored the red Fiesta line.

In 1936, at a show in Pittsburgh, the Homer Laughlin China Company revolutionized the American dinner table with its introduction of a new line of casual dinnerware appropriately named Fiesta. Its design was a remarkable departure from most manufacturers' mere imitations of formal dinnerware. The two significant factors were the streamlined shape with concentric circles that exemplified art deco style and the vibrant colors. My mother was one of the millions of women who happily added the confetti colors to their own dinner tables.

Fiesta's debut was the result of careful research and planning. As one employee recalls, "The final selection of five colors was a more difficult job because we had developed hundreds of tone values and hues." Eventually, visually appealing curves with a concentric band of rings was selected as the hallmark style and the colors chosen were red, cobalt blue, ivory, yellow, and light green. Turquoise was added as a choice the next year, and these six colors are what is now referred to as "vintage" Fiesta.

The original red has a colorful history of its own. During the years of World War II, the sale of uranium oxide was controlled by the government; and the Homer Laughlin company was no longer allowed to purchase the ingredient for its signature brilliant orange-red glaze. Thus, as advertising stated, "red went off to war" and that glaze was discontinued until March 1959. This notoriety added even more to the red's popularity. The manufacturer, anticipating the public's preference for the red and because the red pieces required a separate kiln, originally priced the red higher than the other colors. Since fewer products were produced in that color, red is still desirable with collectors today.

As I explained to my friend, when I collect pieces of red Fiestaware, in addition to having an excuse for visiting flea markets and garage sales, I collect many fond memories.

SETTING THE TABLE

For those interested in collecting Fiesta dinnerware in any color, the following information may be helpful.

COLORS

Collectors use color as the first step in determining the value of a Fiesta piece. The three classifications of colors are based on the time period of their introduction to the marketplace.

•*Vintage:* These include the original red, cobalt blue, ivory, yellow, light green, and turquoise.

•*Fifties Colors:* Added to the line in 1951 were forest green, rose, chartreuse, and gray. The earlier light green, cobalt blue, and ivory were retired. In 1959, medium green, one of the most desirable colors in today's collectors' market, was introduced. Rose, gray, chartreuse, and forest green were discontinued that same year. After sixteen years, red was reintroduced.

•*Post-1986:* Contemporary colors, including such new choices as seamist, persimmon, sapphire, lilac, and others, are referred to as "new" Fiesta. These provide great style with a minimum of expense.

IDENTIFICATION

•*Trademarks:* Four trademarks were used by the company to identify early products. By 1940, the word "genuine" had been added because of frequent imitation.

•*Unmarked:* Some products that were never marked include special promotional pieces, produced between 1939 and 1943.

•*Kiln marks:* Vintage color pieces were fired on "sagger" pins in the kiln, which created three small, glaze-free spots on the bottom of a piece. No new pieces have been fired in that manner.

•*Rims:* The bottom rims of new pieces, as well as some vintage pieces, always have a wiped foot, so

Collectible Fiesta dinnerware is displayed in this photograph by Jessie Walker.

the lack of glaze on the bottom rim is not a final indication of age.

OTHER DISTINGUISHING FEATURES

•*Size:* The clay formula in contemporary Fiesta is different from the vintage line and shrinks more when it is fired. Thus, vintage pieces are slightly larger than their contemporary counterparts.

•*Shape:* Not all vintage pieces, for example, the two-pint jug, have been reproduced in the contemporary lines, so identify the shape of your piece according to when it was made.

•*Color:* The new lead-free glazes do not have the same brilliance as the vintage glazes.

CARING FOR VINTAGE AND FIFTIES FIESTA

Use a mild soap and hand-wash these pieces. Lemon-scented detergents and rinse agents can cause a rainbow effect to appear on the glaze that is impossible to remove.

Berry-Sticky

Kathleen Clark

When summer sizzled
   and hazy skies buzzed,
I'd follow the dusty path
   to the backyard berry patch.
It didn't matter that flies or honey bees
   had tasted the ruby nectar before me.
My skinny arms and lanky legs
   bled a patchwork red
    from thorns and vines,
   but I didn't mind.
One for the bucket, two for me.
The sun-warmed berries popped
   so easily between my cheeks;
   each sticky, sweet, sugary treat
Slipping slowly down my chin
   left a purple-y grin.
One for the bucket, two for me.

FROM *Blueberries*

Robert Frost

"You ought to have seen what I saw on my way
To the village, through Mortenson's pasture today:
Blueberries as big as the end of your thumb,
Real sky-blue, and heavy, and ready to drum
In the cavernous pail of the first one to come!
And all ripe together, not some of them green
And some of them ripe! You ought to have seen!"

"I wish I knew half what the flock of them know
Of where all the berries and other things grow,
Cranberries in bogs and raspberries on top
Of the boulder-strewn mountain,
   and when they will crop.
I met them one day and each had a flower
Stuck into his berries as fresh as a shower. . . ."

Highbush blueberries are ripe for picking. Photograph by William H. Johnson.

HANDMADE HEIRLOOM

Lois Winston

APRONS

When I think back to my childhood in the 1950s, in my mind I always see the women in my family wearing aprons. No matter the task—cooking, cleaning, washing dishes, hanging the laundry, gardening—my mother, grandmothers, and aunts attacked each household chore with an apron tied around their waists. As did all my friends' mothers. Back then, aprons were a *de rigueur* part of a woman's wardrobe, not to mention a standard "mom" gift for birthdays, Christmas, and Mother's Day. Sometimes they were purchased; more often, they were handmade and embellished with embroidery, lace, smocking, or other handiwork.

Beginning in fourth grade, all the girls in my elementary school were required to take home economics. Our first sewing project was a gingham half-apron, which we embellished with cross-stitch. Over the course of that semester, I mastered hand-sewing, simple embroidery, and the sewing machine. More importantly, though, no longer would I have to wear an adult apron, tied awkwardly under my arms to keep me from tripping on the hem and sash. At the end of the course, I had an apron of my own.

The apron did not become commonplace until the thirteenth century when blacksmiths donned leather aprons to protect themselves from the hot metals and sparks of the forge. Today, metal smiths and welders still wear aprons for protection, although they have replaced leather with more protective synthetic materials.

Eventually, more people began wearing aprons to protect both themselves and their clothing. Fishermen found that wool aprons not only kept them dry but kept their clothes free of fish smells. Aprons served multiple purposes for women who used them for both cleaning and gathering items.

At one time a person's occupation could be discerned from the color and pattern of his apron. Gardeners, spinners, weavers, and garbage collectors wore blue aprons. Butlers wore green.

Most women had a kitchen drawer devoted to their apron collection, wearing variously styled aprons for different household chores.

Butchers wore blue stripes. Cobblers wore what was known as "black flag" aprons, which protected them from the black wax they used. English barbers were known as "checkered apron men." Stonemasons wore white.

Although white was traditionally the color of aprons worn by house servants, upper class Victorian women also wore white aprons. However, instead of the simple, utilitarian aprons of their maids, these Victorian ladies spent hours embellishing fine white linen with intricate embroidery and handmade lace and tatting. The aprons, often works of art in themselves, were worn, not for protection from the messiness of household tasks, but as a symbol of domestic pride and a showcase for their talents.

Prior to the Depression, most aprons were made of white cotton or linen. With the onset of the Depression, both materials and money became scarce. Women were forced to make do

Red farm animal pairs strut across the hem of a navy gingham apron.
Apron design and construction courtesy of DMC. Photograph by Jerry Koser.

with whatever fabrics they could scrounge. Aprons, like quilts, were often made from feed and flour sacks. The use of these patterned fabrics signified a turning point in the appearance of aprons. After the Depression, calicoes became popular fabrics for aprons. By the 1940s, many aprons featured large floral print fabrics.

In the 1940s and 1950s, women were often pictured wearing aprons in magazine advertisements and later on television commercials. The apron-clad housewife became the emblematic salesperson for everything from kitchen appliances to frozen foods. Most women had a kitchen drawer devoted to their apron collection, wearing variously styled aprons for different household chores. Women embellished their aprons with rickrack, buttons, ribbons, beads, and lace. Aprons featuring printed pictures of popular tourist attractions became a standard souvenir item for women to purchase while on vacation.

In the early 1970s, the hostess apron, complete with ruffles, had a brief period of popularity. Now, however, most women only bother with an apron for a specific messy task, such as baking. Often, a father is the family member seen wearing a simple canvas apron while flipping burgers at the grill. Today aprons are mostly seen in restaurants on waiters and chefs. But during my last visit to an antique mall, I noticed that reproductions of old aprons were being sold in several booths.

Patterns for aprons can still be found at fabric stores. To embellish a gingham apron with cross-stitch, choose a fabric with a small check. Use the gingham as a grid for the cross-stitch, working over either one square of the check or a block of four squares for each cross-stitch. Designs for cross-stitch patterns can be found in books at craft and needlework shops. Make your selection from simple patterns that work best when stitching on gingham. Use an embroidery hoop to keep the fabric taut as you stitch.

The popularity of aprons is returning in today's fast-paced world. Even though its practical function is no longer a daily necessity, an apron can add individuality and old-fashioned charm to entertaining.

Lois Winston is a freelance writer and designer whose work appears regularly in craft and women's magazines. Her home is in New Jersey.

BITS & PIECES

$\mathcal{S}$ummer afternoon—summer afternoon; to me those have always been the two most beautiful words in the English language.

—*Henry James*

$\mathcal{S}$ummer, so much too beautiful to stay.

—*Elinor Wylie*

$\mathcal{A}$ healthy man, indeed, is the complement of the seasons, and in winter, summer is in his heart.

—*Henry David Thoreau*

$\mathcal{I}$'d give all wealth that years have piled,
The slow result of Life's decay,
To be once more a little child
For one bright summer-day.

—*Lewis Carroll*

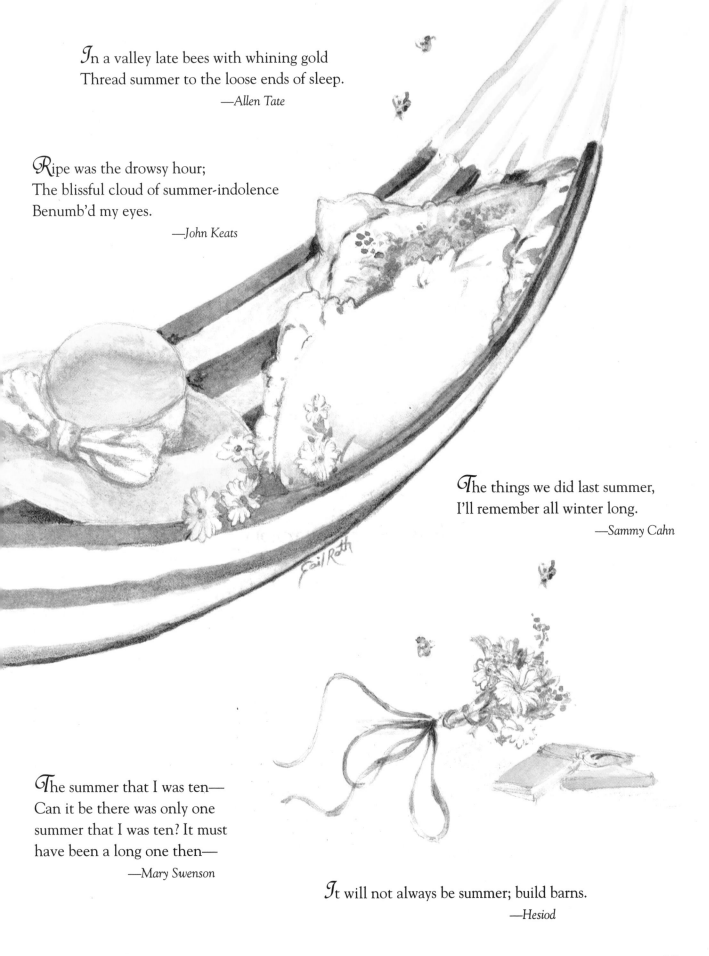

In a valley late bees with whining gold
Thread summer to the loose ends of sleep.
—*Allen Tate*

Ripe was the drowsy hour;
The blissful cloud of summer-indolence
Benumb'd my eyes.
—*John Keats*

The things we did last summer,
I'll remember all winter long.
—*Sammy Cahn*

The summer that I was ten—
Can it be there was only one
summer that I was ten? It must
have been a long one then—
—*Mary Swenson*

It will not always be summer; build barns.
—*Hesiod*

35

My mother, who hates thunderstorms,
Holds up each summer day and shakes
It out suspiciously, lest swarms
Of grape-dark clouds are lurking there....
—PHILIP LARKIN

July Afternoon
Roslyn Davidson

The rain blew up from the south,
Filtering through the trees,
Skippping across the barn roof
On tiny tin hooves.

Nature's raucous celebration
Of nourishing, cleansing,
Was a power presentation
Starring sound and light.

*Black-eyed Susans are washed by a gentle
rain. Photograph by Daniel Dempster.*

The Romance of Daisies

Theresa H. Morr

What springs to mind when you think of daisies? Not the perfect, cultivated kind, but the humble little flower known botanically as *Leucanthemum vulgare*, or more simply as the oxeye or field daisy. Perhaps, like me, when you think of daisies you will remember how the unpretentious flower had a way of revealing the truth of many a heart's desire.

Those sweet, unrushed days are bygones, but like sun-drenched buttercups and dandelions, these native daisies flourish in wild abandon across America's countryside, forever gladdening our hearts. It is what daisies do best.

While some folks consider the field daisy a pesky weed deserving of a good foot-stomping, this homespun beauty with its familiar nodding white rays and bright yellow center is an easy plant to love once you get to know it. My southern Maryland daisies quietly tame the land along once-barren roadsides, thrive gloriously in meadows and fields, and stretch languorously heavenward on hillsides and along creek edges and places in between.

An anonymous author once wrote, "If I had my life to live over, I would climb more mountains, swim more rivers, and watch more sunsets. I would eat more ice cream. I would go places and do things. I'd travel lighter than I have. I would start barefooted earlier in the spring and stay that way later in the fall. I would ride on merry-go-rounds. I'd pick more daisies."

Bright-eyed field daisies, the oxeyes, may not be as favored in floral and garden shops or as sought after as the queen of the garden, the red rose. But in its calm, unspoiled way, the delightful little daisy will long endure across the land as it always has.

Oxeye daisies dance across a hillside in the Willamette Valley of Marion County, Oregon. Photograph by Steve Terrill.

FROM MY GARDEN JOURNAL

Lisa Ragan

BLACK-EYED SUSANS

On lazy summer afternoons I can often be found sitting on my back porch with a good book. This is a well-cultivated habit that I first began developing in childhood. I loved to read as a young girl, and I have happy summer memories of lying on a quilt in my parents' backyard and reading to my heart's content. I especially loved *Little House on the Prairie* by Laura Ingalls Wilder, and I used to imagine what it might be like to be Laura, a little girl growing up on the prairie. In my romantic imagination I saw myself riding a palomino through meadows filled with wildflowers of every color. Although my life today includes no horses and no wildflower-filled prairies, I do enjoy wildflowers in my own backyard garden. One of my favorites is the black-eyed Susan, a hardy bloomer that can bring a touch of the meadowlands wherever it's planted.

BACKGROUND

The black-eyed Susan hails from North America east of the Mississippi River, where it has grown wild for an untold number of years. A member of the Asteraceae family and cousin to sunflowers, the black-eyed Susan was once classified in the Compositae family; some sources may still use the old family name. The common name of black-eyed Susan may denote several different species of the *Rudbeckia* genus, including *R. hirta*, *R. fulgida*, and *R. triloba*. Other common names can include brown-eyed Susan and orange coneflower. The plant was given its name in the eighteenth century by the botanist Carolus Linnaeus, the father of botanical nomenclature.

CHARACTERISTICS

The black-eyed Susan is a hardy plant and a reliable

bloomer that produces hairy, oval leaves of dark green and flower heads of bright golden yellow petals surrounding a center cone of dark brown. The daisy-like blossoms usually open to two-and-a-half-inches wide and range in color from lemony yellow to a deep gold with centers ranging from dark brown to burgundy and even green. A type of coneflower, the black-eyed Susan can be grown as a perennial, annual, or even a biennial, depending upon the part of the country in which it is planted. Black-eyed Susans begin their blooming period in midsummer and typically continue through autumn until the first hard frost. The plant is drought tolerant once well established and performs exceedingly well as a cut flower.

VARIETIES

Black-eyed Susans have been celebrated throughout North America for centuries and have inspired hybridizers to create many ornamental varieties suitable for the everyday gardener. One of the most popular is *R. fulgida* var. *sullivantii* Goldsturm, a classic-looking black-eyed Susan that produces a "gold storm" (the English translation of its German name) of blossoms in mid- to late summer. Goldsturm stretches its hairy green stems to heights of about two feet and fills out to about one-and-a-half feet in width. Growing a little bit taller to heights of three to four feet, *R. hirta* features flowers that range in hue from golden orange to burgundy and stems and leaves that are *hirta*, Latin for rough and hairy.

One of the most desirable cultivars of *R. hirta* is Indian Summer, which produces six- to nine-inch golden yellow flowers atop stiff, hairy stems that branch out in width to three or four feet. One of the most unusual black-eyed Susan cultivars is *R. nitida* Herbstsonne, a six-foot giant with vivid yellow flower petals around a

green center cone. Herbstsonne usually requires staking to keep its magnificent form.

CULTIVATION

Whichever variety of this dependable plant gardeners select, most have relatively simple requirements for cultivation. Black-eyed Susans can be grown from seed or by dividing established plants in the spring. The Goldsturm cultivar can only be grown from seed, but performs admirably in many types of soil conditions. Black-eyed Susans should be planted in full sun, although many types can handle partial shade. The plant will grow in almost any type of soil except soggy, wet soil. Gardeners should also note that soil that is too rich can sometimes yield floppy plants. Black-eyed Susans need plenty of water when young, but can tolerate drier conditions once established.

Removing spent blossoms frequently, also known as "deadheading," throughout the blooming season will encourage even more flowering and will help control the plant's tendency to self-sow. Some gardeners choose to leave the seed heads on the plant throughout the winter as food for wild birds.

Perhaps the best news of all is that no particular pests or diseases plague the black-eyed Susan.

The black-eyed Susans in my own garden grow against a backdrop of ornamental grasses and alongside purple coneflowers and bee balm, which all together create a tiny meadow of country wildflowers that have been tamed for a life in town. My little bit of prairie provides a serene summer vista from the comfort of my glider as I settle in for a good read.

Lisa Ragan, with the help of her son, Trenton, tends a small but mighty garden in Nashville, Tennessee.

Milkweed Pod

Prentice Baker

Six deep-woods, scarlet tanagers in a group,
Conferring formerly with the wounded quail,
Rose through the beech boughs over the quail's coop
So urgently the beechnuts fell like hail.
I found, when I shut the screen door to the stoop,
A milkweed seed-pod in the water pail.
A long time then I stared into the sky
Over the sorghum tassels, letting day die
And green tomatoes ripening on the sill
Dull into shadow. Once a whippoorwill

Cried in the bottom. Drifting out of dusk,
This hesitant, silk-furred insubstantial husk
Sat on a surface not designed to bear it,
Desperate, and unable to declare it.
Thoughtful, I bore it to the sill to dry
In the uncertain thought that it might fly.
The massive cane, so green as to seem black,
Clashed leaves, and made such stir as drew me back.
Lampless, inscrutable, night rose before me blind,
But the wonder of wandering things was in my mind.

> THE REAL THINGS OF LIFE THAT ARE THE COMMON POSSESSION OF US ALL ARE OF THE GREATEST VALUE—WORTH FAR MORE THAN MOTOR CARS OR RADIOS, MORE THAN LANDS OR MONEY—AND OUR WHOLE STORE OF THESE WONDERFUL RICHES MAY BE REVEALED TO US BY SUCH A COMMON, BEAUTIFUL THING AS A WILD SUNFLOWER.
>
> LAURA INGALLS WILDER

Hayfield

Dean Robbins

My wandering a country road
Led to men harvesting a field
Where baled hay became a load.
Their cattle would reap the morning's yield.
The elder steered his tractor straight;
It pulled a wagon close behind.
Two younger men were tempting fate,
Though neither seemed to mind,

By stacking bales much too high,
Then climbing ever higher,
As if they meant to touch the sky
Before the noon sun turned to fire.
But, no, they simply gathered hay
To store for times when snow will fly—
As noble an effort in its way
As any man's reach for the sky.

Everlasting pea flowers and thistle seeds are illuminated by sunlight in the Columbia River Gorge National Scenic Area, Oregon. Photograph by Steve Terrill.

REMEMBER WHEN

Adeline Roseberg

PAPA'S STORE

My parents were both born in Sweden, married in the Glory community of Aitkin County, Minnesota, and lived all their married lives on the same place. Papa was twenty when he got "America fever" and came to this country. Now, when I think of it, I marvel at all he was able to accomplish—a new language to learn, and self re-education in reading, writing, and everything. I can't help wondering how he managed so much—farm, store, post office, cream hauling, and a family of seven daughters and four sons. Yet he found time for church, school, and community. He was Sunday school superintendent for twenty-five years or more, and built the fires in the church all those years, too. And he was almost always on the school and town boards.

Maybe it was that hour alone each morning—before he called the family to get up—that gave Papa strength for the day. He always got up at five, built the fires, put coffee on, read a bit in the Bible, then had a little time for thought and meditation as he sipped that wonderful cup of coffee. He brought Mama a cup of coffee to enjoy before she got out of bed. Then he'd call us kids. I often lay awake those early mornings, listening to the comforting noises downstairs and knowing it would be awhile before we'd have to get up.

Before the days of the automobile, the country store was vital. I remember the old hitching post, where folks tied up their horses when they came to do their trading. In those days, folks said "trading" rather than shopping because much of it actually was trading. They would bring their cases or pails of eggs and jars of homemade butter to exchange for stuff from the store.

I can remember we sold almost everything,

Papa was quick to ask folks in for coffee before they set off on their homeward journey.

---

not just groceries. We had dry goods—bib overalls, blue shirts, Rockford socks, canvas gloves, gingham, calico, and oilcloth. And there was hardware—nails, screws, bolts, mower parts, and such things. And feed—bran, cracked corn, and even oyster shells for the chickens.

We had no fresh meats, though, because we did not have refrigeration. But there were always salt pork and bacon slabs, summer sausage, pickled herring, and salt herring. We also had gift items, too, like fancy plates, vases, and beads, plus things for the ladies, like hairpins and hairnets. No detergents or soap powders, but stacks of good old laundry soap and big yellow bars of Fels Naptha.

Country folks could not go too far to cure their ills in those days, either. So we had a supply of medicine to take care of most anything.

Many things were sold in bulk—wooden

boxes of dried apples, apricots, prunes, and raisins. There was a big barrel of granulated sugar that swung on hinges from beneath the counter. And the glass case with compartments for different brands of whole-berry coffee.

We had scoops of various sizes for weighing a purchase before it was put into a brown paper bag. I remember the huge round cheese and the cutter that clamped down to cut various-sized wedges.

We also pumped vinegar from the old vinegar barrel into containers folks brought in, especially during pickling season. The

A potbelly stove warms a country store. Photograph from Retrofile/H. Armstrong Roberts.

kerosene container had a pump, too, with a place to hang a can. Papa always checked to see if the spout of the can had the little top screwed on. If it didn't, he would put a small potato on the end to keep the kerosene from spilling on the way home.

We didn't keep gasoline on hand until after we'd gotten our first car—that grand old Studebaker. We kept a barrel in a shed, turned on a spigot to fill a gallon can, put a funnel in the gas tank of the car, and poured in the gas.

Papa was quick to ask folks in for coffee before they set off on their homeward journey. Many walked long distances. Others came from

far away with horse and buggy or wagon in summer and sleigh in winter. The coffee pot stayed on the old wood stove in the house, and Papa expected Mama to be ready to serve a lunch to anybody at a moment's notice, at any time of day. And she did.

With the coming of the automobile and better roads, the country store lost its importance. But it had served the pioneers at a time when it was needed, and it served them well.

A longer version of this article originally appeared in the September 4, 1971, issue of The Farmer.

Tenantry
(POLK COUNTY, TENNESSEE)
George Scarbrough

Always in transit
we were temporarily
in exile,
each new place seeming
after a while
and for a while
our home.

Because no matter
how far we traveled
on the edge of strangeness
in a small county,
the earth ran before us
down red clay roads
blurred with summer dust,
banked with winter mud.

It was the measurable,
pleasurable earth
that was home.
Nobody who loved it
could ever really be alien.
Its tough clay, deep loam,
hill rocks, small flowers
were always the signs
of a homecoming.

We wound down through them
to them,
and the house we came to,
whispering with dead hollyhocks
or once in spring
sill-high in daisies,
was unimportant.
Wherever it stood,
it stood in earth,
and the earth welcomed us,
open, gateless,
one place as another.

And each place seemed
after a while
and for a while
our home:
because the county
was only a mansion
kind of dwelling
in which there were many
rooms.
We only moved from one
room to another,
getting acquainted
with the whole house.

And always the earth
was the new floor under us,
the blue pinewoods the walls
rising around us,
the windows the openings
in the blue trees
through which we glimpsed,
always farther on,
sometimes beyond the river,
the real wall of the mountain,
in whose shadow
for a little while
we assumed ourselves safe,
secure and comfortable
as happy animals
in an unvisited lair:

which is why perhaps
no house we ever lived in
stood behind a fence,
no door we ever opened
had a key.

It was beautiful like that.
For a little while.

An open gate welcomes visitors at a cabin near Story, Indiana. Photograph by Daniel Dempster.

47

One Day

Beverly McLoughland

One day is like another to a cow—
     the long and languid grazing in the meadow,
     the patient chewing of the cud,
     the gazing out upon the world with quiet eyes—
the leisurely turning
of the whole green meadow
into a wide and flowing river of milk.

The Individual Cow

Dorothy B. Taggart

At milking time
The cows come heavy to the barn.
They seem to know
By weight or certain light of day
When time is up.
But this one cow,
White and some black,
Would stay behind
Just now and then,
And we would go
Down the cow path,
Through the birches
And the bull briers
And the shad flies
To the brook.
There she would stand,
Quite statuesque,

Hoof-deep in muck,
Until she heard
Us say, "Come, Boss,"
Or felt the switch
Upon her rump.
Then she would turn
Deliberately,
Swish her tail and
Plod up the path,
With us behind,
In slow cadence
To the barn.
Our father said,
"That stubborn cow
Is just too dumb to mention."
But Mama seemed to understand
She just needed the attention.

Young calves receive special care in a painting entitled
FEEDING THE CALVES *by Thomas James Lloyd (1849-1910).*
Image from Fine Art Photographic Library Ltd.,
London/Antony Mitchell Fine Paintings.

The Measure of a Man
L. A. Davidson

My father built a bluebird house
    on top the clothesline post
    and laid a gray cocoon
    on a kitchen window ledge.

He brought wild roses in his hat
    when June sun warmed the days,

before the memory had yet faded
    of Johnny-jump-ups in his hands.

His whistle marked a steady stride
    from pre-dawn till after dark,
    with silent pauses here and there
    for sunrise, sunset, meadowlark.

My Father's Hands
Mrs. Paul E. King

It is fun to make hay in the summer
    And ride on the wagon piled high
With the fragrant and sweet-smelling stuff
    That almost reaches the sky.
And the reins that guide the big horses
    I proudly hold tight, like a man,
While my father sits right up close to me
    And guides us all home with his hand.

The night is a time of pure magic,
    When whippoorwills come out to sing;
I love to sit in the moonlight
    And listen to everything.
I'm not afraid when the hoot owl
    Calls "Who, who, who, who?" in the land,
For my father sits right up close to me
    And keeps a warm grip on my hand.

I love to go nutting in autumn
    And plow long, deep furrows in leaves,
Then climb up the slender wild grapevine
    And swing near the tops of the trees.
And it is so much more fun when a fellow
    Has with him another man,
When that man is a little boy's father,
    Who keeps a tight grip on his hand.

A summer cornfield provides a green background for a colorful perennial garden. Photograph by William H. Johnson.

The Old Tin Dipper

Ellen Chambers

It hung with its dents
    on the side of our well,
Where Father had strung it,
    one hot summer spell,
Calling his children
    from green-willow play
To come have a sip
    on a red summer day.

While he pumped us a stream,
    there was sweat on his face,
And I watched you with the dipper,
    hold it in place.
And the three of us shared
    a quick gulp from its rim.
How you and I worshipped
    a father like him.

On the days he was working
    the fields far away,
He somehow seemed near,
    in a slow dipper's sway;
He seemed there to bless us
    whenever we'd drink,
And somewhere he smiled,
    when we'd lift it, I think.

As the dipper grew older
    and time took its toll,
Its handle grew twisted,
    and bent was its bowl,
But in spite of its tarnish,
    it held, crystal clear,
the face of a father,
    who somewhere was near.

For Father was wise,
    and he so loved the land,
He gave us this tool
    to hold in our hand,
That we filled and we spilled
    to a sweet overflow,
And drank in his memory,
    wherever he'd go.

Strawberries overflow their baskets near an old pump. Photograph by H. Abernathy/ H. Armstrong Roberts.

A Letter to My Farmer Father

Kathy Smith Anthenat

Happy Father's Day, Dad. I just want to say "thank you."

Perhaps you are disappointed that none of us chose to follow in your footsteps. Perhaps you are a bit lonely as you sit in the front room and wait for needed rains and loved children, both of whom are far too elusive.

We grew up watching the cloud of dust that was you and your tractor at work and heard you come in, finally, long after dark. We saw you gazing at the skies, "guestimating" if the coming rain would hold off long enough to bale and haul the hay that was already cut and raked. Too often it did not.

We watched you worry about bills at the end of the second dry year in a row and did not bother making wishes from the wish book. The next year would have been a bumper crop, if only the fields had dried up enough to get a tractor in there to harvest them.

We also watched you smile with contentment as you checked out a beautiful field of sweet clover that only a farmer could appreciate. We *oohed* with delight at the nest of orphaned baby bunnies that you brought home from the hay field.

We watched you pull school buses out of mud and strangers' cars out of ditches with your tractor and learned from what you told the grateful stranger when he tried to pay you: "Just pass it on."

You brought us cold watermelons, homemade ice cream, horehound candy, and a thousand other things for which we probably never said "thank you."

We left for other towns, other states, other lifestyles. But we have never, ever forgotten. And although we decided not be farmers, our heritage is cherished: daughters and sons of a proud American farmer, homegrown in Flora, Illinois.

Although we now sit in college classes, business meetings, and suburban homes, lessons from the farm still apply. We learned to proceed with caution around the snakes and poison ivy on the farm, but we never let them detour us from exploring the wonders of the woods and creeks. In today's world there are still snakes and evils, and there are still wonders. We will proceed with caution.

On the farm, you had to speak up if you wanted to get the chicken platter before it was empty of the mashed potatoes. Today we still know how to speak up—to get the prize job assignment or a thorough explanation from our child's doctor.

We learned that if you talk all the time you will never hear the whippoorwill. And that if you want to enjoy a blackberry cobbler, you have to pay the price: briers and chiggers.

Thank you for teaching us how to hold an important decision in our fist like a ball of dirt and test it to see if it is ready for our plow. Thank you for adversity that kept us from growing up too spindly like a tomato seedling that has had too much water and not enough hot sun. Thank you for shouldering duties in life, like burying the family dog, until we were old enough to do them. Thank you for caring more about the cleanliness of our morals than of our faces. Thank you for the type of childhood which seems to be getting squeezed out in the technological shuffle. Thank you for my appreciation of quiet moments, spring rains, and cedar Christmas trees.

Today I celebrate my good fortune in having you for a father.

A meandering stream flows toward a ranch on Antelope Flats at daybreak at Grand Teton National Park, Wyoming. Photograph by Terry Donnelly.

Dad

Samuel Harden Stille

Not much for style
Or fixing up,
But all the while,
In sun or storm,
He stands upon the hill
Of memory
Like an oak.

Through storm and sun
He taught us,
As he was taught,
To stand erect—
Face the wind
And storms of life
Like the oak,
His counterpart.

Man of the soil,
Kind but firm,
Friend of honest toil,
He sought thus to earn
His daily bread
And place
Upon the hill.

Everything I ever learned as a small boy came from my father. And I never found anything he ever told me to be wrong or worthless. The simple lessons he taught me are as sharp and clear in my mind as if I had heard them only yesterday. Men like my father cannot die. They are with me still, real in memory as they were in flesh, loving and beloved forever. How green was my valley then.

—Philip Dunne, from *How Green Was My Valley*

Pioneer Spirit

Margaret H. Hasbargen

My father measured countless miles
Behind a one-horse plow;
By hand he fashioned fields of corn,
Set shocks of grain, and milked each cow;
By hand he fought intruding weeds
And heaped hay high into the mow.

He bartered youth and strength for lines
Etched deeper in his brow;
Before recurrent drought or flood
His spirit would not bow;
And from this moment's retrospect
My heart salutes him now.

*A cabin rests beside Tangle Lake in Alaska.
Photograph by Dennis Frates.*

My Father's Philosophy

D. A. Hoover

My father had a creed for life
He taught to everyone:
"Look forward to your pleasant times
Until your work is done.
When you have finished every task,
Your mind will be at rest;
Life's good times are the sweetest
When you've done your very best."

I have kept this lesson in my heart
As seasons come and go;
And every test I've put it to,
I have always found it so.

My Father's Way

Raymond Kresensky

My father walked a straighter way
Than I could ever find. He'd say
When we were lost among the trees
Along the creek, "God planted these,
Not to confuse or leave you lost.
He left a way you could have crossed
Straight through your little forest here,
But you were blinded by false fear."

My father's path was always straight;
Up the hill or down, no change in gait.
He went along knowing the end
Was not determined by the bend
Or turn or rock-strewn brambled course,
But by the lonely power and force
That led him over plain and hill
Nearer to God—now, nearer still.

*An outcrop provides a breathtaking view of
Cedar Creek Valley at Petit Jean State Park,
Arkansas. Photograph by Terry Donnelly.*

59

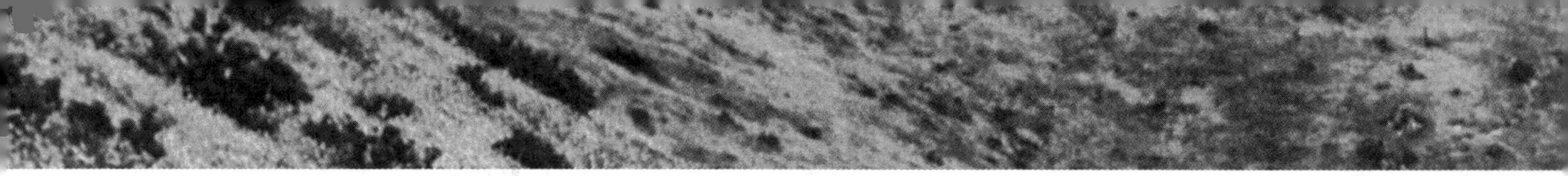

COMPANIONSHIP

Craig E. Sathoff

I have no fond companion
As valued as my son.
I marvel at the spritely course
His youthful vigor runs.

For when it comes a holiday,
And I have time to spare,
We start before the rooster crows
With things we two will share.

Just as the sun is stretching forth,
We're gaily on our way
To try to catch a string of fish
Before the noon of day.

A nature hike, a round of catch,
A game of horseshoes too,
And more that we can think to do
Before the day is through.

When finally the sun has set,
And all is calm and still,
We've chess to play and soap to carve
And many a tale to tell.

It is a great companionship
That we have come to share;
And though my muscles ache a bit,
It beats the rocking chair.

A FATHER'S PRAYER

Reginald Holmes

I do not ask for wealth untold,
For glory, and for fame.
I ask to live a life that's free
From envy and from shame.

I do not ask that skies above
Are always clear and bright,
But for a little star to shine
And guide me through the night.

I do not ask that men bestow
Their flattery and praise,
But for a loyal friend or two
Who will be true always.

Please let me live an honest life
Without pretense or sham;
And let me be the kind of man
My children think I am.

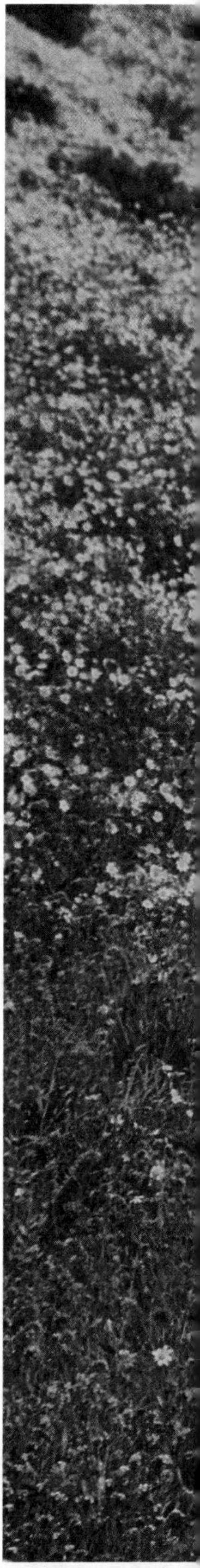

*Horses trot on a flowering hillside near Temblor Range
in California. Photograph by Londie G. Padelsky.*

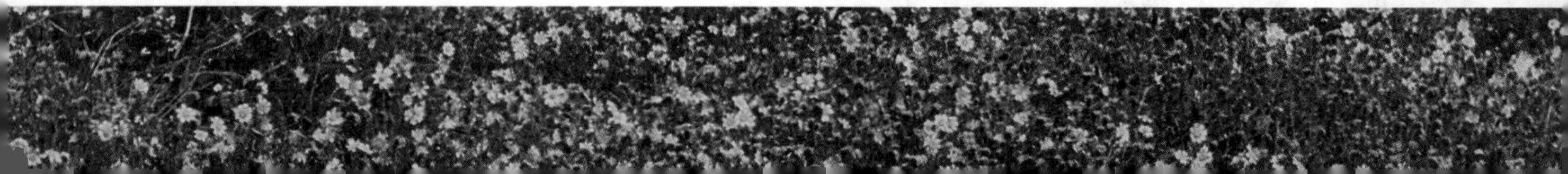

SLICE OF LIFE

Edna Jaques

THE FARMER

He found his joy in common things.
    He ate the royal bread of kings;
His birthright was a quiet soul,
    A healthy body, clean and whole.
A battered hat of straw his crown;
    His kingdom was a field of brown.

And there within his fair domain
    He held the sceptre of his reign.
The seasons served him bed and board;
    The sun and rain his overlord.
The germ of life in seed and flower,
    The living symbols of his power.

He tilled the soil its wealth to find,
    His field, the servant of mankind;
He felt the pulse of Nature's blood
    And spoke the tongue she understood.
He dwelt in bondage fast, yet he
    Was monarch of his destiny.

Artist Robert Duncan began painting at age eleven, when his grandmother gave him his first set of oil paints. During summers spent on his grandparents' ranch, he grew to love the rural life. Today, Robert, his wife, the youngest of his six children, and a lively assortment of farm animals live in the little town of Midway, Utah.

DEVOTIONS FROM THE HEART

Pamela Kennedy

But he that received seed into the good ground is he that heareth the word, and understandeth it; which also beareth fruit, and bringeth forth, some an hundredfold, some sixty, some thirty.
—Matthew 13:23

GOOD SOIL

It was just about three and the kindergartners at the girls' school where I teach lined up behind their teachers. Then they marched, backpacks bouncing, to the gate to meet their parents. Each little girl held a paper cup in her hands and each cup held soil and a bean plant about five inches tall. The leafy green stalks waved in the afternoon breeze. I smiled, recalling the year my younger son had sprouted beans in paper cups to fulfill a science project about plant growth. After carefully tending his seeds for weeks, nurturing them with a variety of ingredients, he produced a little bean plantation with specimens of various heights and vigor. That is, until the morning the project was due. We rose that day to discover sixteen paper cups, each containing a stubby, leafless green stalk. Ebony, our big black cat, sat purring on the floor, surrounded by tattered bean leaves. Fortunately our son had some graphs, photos, and an understanding teacher, so all was not lost. But it made me think about growing things—and about faith.

When Jesus taught His disciples using the parable of the sower, He used an object familiar in their agrarian society. Everybody knew about seeds. People planted them, watered them, cultivated them, and then waited for them to grow. Jesus said that God's Word is a lot like seed. It falls upon the soil of our hearts and, depending upon the condition of that soil, it takes root and grows. Sometimes the soil is hard and unyielding and then the seed is eaten by birds. Other times the soil nurtures the seed for a little while, and then, because the soil is shallow or full of weeds, the sprouted seed withers and dies. But then Jesus

Dear Lord of seeds and soil, help me to prepare my heart so that Your Word may always find a place to grow and multiply there.

talked about good soil, soil that yields many times more than what was planted. This soil produces healthy, abundant plants.

I looked again at the kindergartners with their paper cups. They held their little plants carefully. For weeks they had tenderly watered their seeds, set them in the sunshine, protected them from pests; and, now, their little bean seeds had produced leafy, green shoots.

What an illustration of Jesus' parable!

Children gather lessons from nature. Photograph by Londie G. Padelsky.

When we hear the good seed of God's Word through our own Bible study, or the teaching of another, we each have a choice. Will it fall upon hard heart-soil, sucked dry by the concerns of today, cracked and dusty from fretting about tomorrow? Will it lie there untended, waiting to be stolen by the birds of disbelief? Will it spring up quickly, fueled by early enthusiasm, only to wither when we become overwhelmed with problems or worries? Or will this newly planted seed of faith fall on receptive soil, softened by humility, watered with the encouragement of prayer, exposed to the light of study and meditation, protected from the pests of doubt and worry? If we choose to keep our heart-soil soft, tender, and well-nourished, Jesus says we can expect to produce even more faith. That little seed of hope will grow.

And the wonder of it all is that it doesn't just remain alone, but produces an abundance that can be shared with others; the hundred, sixty, or thirty times Jesus spoke about. When our faith grows, we have enough to give to others. We can offer a word of encouragement or comfort. We can reach out with generosity and grace, lifting someone else's spirits, building faith. We can overflow with the blessings of our own harvest and, in thanks, nourish our families, friends, and even strangers. Those seeds of faith are important, but they need to be planted in the willing soil of our hearts before we can enjoy the blessings of God's bounty.

First Garden

Ellen Chambers

It was early spring when my father's hands
Opened a paper sack
And poured in my palm
    a river of seeds,
Smooth and round and black.

I can see it now, the fresh-cut twig
He snipped for my little hoe,
And the place where he pointed
    for me to start
To make a garden grow.

Only four, I had never planted before,
And my strokes were ragged and bent,
But he crouched to his knees,

And I knew I had pleased,
As he smiled at where the seeds went.

And he told me the story of how the sun
And the rain would nurture the seeds
And how earth played a part,
    with its rich black heart,
To comfort their lives and feed.

And then, tasting an autumn's rich reward
As I chattered about more springs,
I caught the lesson
    my father had taught,
Of patience toward all living things.

Inheritance

Pat Potel

At home when there was handiwork, I often helped my dad.
In his quiet way he made these times the best we ever had.
We'd gather up a vast array of tools and then commence
To rearrange the furnace pipes or build a picket fence
Or make an orange-crate scooter or repair a broken bike
Or fix a clock or concrete walk or anything we'd like.

He taught me how to varnish and to nail and solder too.
We'd saw and plane and sand and paint to turn the old to new.
I loved the patient pride he took with drill and rasp and rule.
His hands were large but deft and quick with even the smallest tool.
And every job he did was done as perfect as could be;
Man's work was what he did the best, and this he taught to me.

I'll never know if Dad had planned these lessons with some aim;
It seemed enough for both of us to simply share what came.
And, childlike, I never thought to question how they'd serve,
But gleaned a truth, a trick, a skill, and held them in reserve.

And then one day my own small son brought even this reward,
When a backyard building project stalled from something untoward.
He solved the problem with a whoop that made my laughter ring:
"We'll find out how," he proudly piped, "My mom knows everything!"

A bouquet of sunflowers in an old milk can stands beside a wagon that has found new purpose as a display place for summer flowers. Photograph by Jessie Walker.

Until you have a son of your own . . . you will never know the joy, the love beyond feeling that resonates in the heart of a father as he looks upon his son. You will never know the sense of honor that makes a man want to be more than he is and to pass something good and hopeful into the hands of his son.

—KENT NERBURN, FROM *LETTERS TO MY SON*

Learning

Roy Z. Kemp

We walk together, my son and I,
Beneath the bright blue band of sky.
He questions me, I question him
Till evening's light begins to dim.

Time passes swiftly—time should creep.
The gulf is wide, the chasm deep;
A father and son—so much between
The two of us, so much unseen,

But deeply felt. There is no word
Descriptive of a sound unheard,
Yet any father in any land
Can feel, can know, can understand.

Father and son, each offering each
Important things that both can teach:
One hearing small-boy thoughts again,
One learning the stranger ways of men.

My Stepfather

J. Darlene Campbell

When I was just a lad,
My mother gave to me
The living image of the kind of man
She hoped I'd one day be.
A man whose gentleness and strength
Were a pillar in times of need,
A man whose words of praise
Met every childish deed.

He was there to guide me
Along the paths of youth;
He was there to teach me
To face the world with truth.
Of all the gifts my mother gave,
Most priceless is the one
Of love and understanding
From the man who calls me "son."

And now I stand before you,
The man you've made of me.
I've come to ask you, Dad,
To thank my mother for me.

Little Sheep Creek flows through a valley in Wallowa County, Oregon. Photograph by Steve Terrill.

FOR THE CHILDREN

Color the Farm

Eileen Spinelli

The pigs are pink.
The barn is red.
There's the tall-wheat yellow
   and a thread
   of orange on
   the barn owl's back.

The fence is white.
The sheep is black.
The earth is brown.
The sky is blue.
The tractor's green.
The corn is too.

Come celebrate
   the country charm
   of summer colors
   on the farm.

LEGENDARY AMERICANS

Maud Dawson and Melinda Rathjen

E. B. WHITE

The publication of a children's novel on October 15, 1952, about a young pig who is befriended by a spider forever changed the field of American children's literature. The E. B. White narrative about Wilbur, the runt of his litter, and the lessons he learns as a member of a barnyard community and about the values taught by his dainty friend Charlotte, the gluttonous rat Templeton, and various other critters readers come to enjoy in *Charlotte's Web* has charmed several generations of American readers. Eudora Welty's review of the new book by White described it as having "grace and humor and praise of life, and the good backbone of succinctness that only the most highly imaginative stories seem to grow." In her conclusion, she states what millions of readers have since also concluded, *Charlotte's Web* "is an adorable book" whose themes examine "life and death, trust and treachery, pleasure and pain, and the passing of time."

White, a graduate of Cornell University, had already established a career as an essayist before the publication of his second novel for young readers. He had begun his career writing for the *New Yorker* and later for *Harper's Magazine*. James Thurber, another writer and friend to White, stated later that White had been the "most valuable person" on the staff of the *New Yorker*. Collections of White's essays, poems, and letters are still in print and avidly read and widely quoted today.

A third area of White's contribution to American literature is in the revision of a writing handbook for students called *The Elements of Style*. Published in 1959, it was reviewed by the *Wall Street Journal* and White was described as "one of the best stylists and most lucid minds in this country."

Elwyn Brooks White was born to Jessie Hart White and Samuel Tilly White in 1899. He was the youngest of six children. His decision to become a writer came early in his life. In a letter written to a brother, he states, "I can remember, really quite distinctly, looking a piece of paper square in the eyes when I was seven or eight years old and thinking 'This is where I belong, this is it'."

NAME: Elwyn Brooks White

BORN: July 11, 1899, Mount Vernon, New York, Westchester County

DIED: October 1, 1985

ACCOMPLISHMENTS: Author of three children's classics, *Stuart Little, Charlotte's Web*, and *Trumpet of the Swan*; respected language stylist; and renowned essayist

AWARDS: Presidential Medal of Freedom, 1963; National Medal for Literature, 1971; a Pulitzer Prize special citation, 1978; Laura Ingalls Wilder Award; and others

The main character of *Stuart Little*, White's first children's book, appeared during a train journey to the Shenandoah Valley many years before White actually completed the manuscript: "While asleep in an upper berth, I dreamed of a small character who had the features of a mouse, was nicely dressed, courageous, and questing."

As the young uncle to eighteen nephews and nieces, White had entertained these children with stories about a mouse that undertakes many adventures. Years later, when the children's librarian at the New York Public Library suggested White consider writing a book for children, his editor at the time encouraged him to complete the Stuart Little tale. Published in 1945, the book was immediately popular. By the end of 1946, the publisher had printed more than 100,000 copies. White explained later that he had learned two things from the experience of writing this first novel for children—that "a writer's own nose is his best guide, and that children can sail easily over the fence that separates reality from make-believe. They go over it like little springboks. A fence that can throw a librarian is as nothing to a child."

After White married Katharine, the fiction editor of the *New Yorker*, they and their family divided their time between New York City and their farm in Maine. Life on this farm provided the inspiration for White's most successful children's book, *Charlotte's Web*. One day, White observed a gray spider laying eggs and placed her and the egg sac in a candy box and took them with him when he returned to New York City. He was delighted when the baby spiders began spinning tiny webs on his dresser. He researched the particular species of spider and gave his famous heroine, Charlotte, her

E. B. White and "Minnie," a dachsund, take a moment to relax. Photograph provided by Cornell University Library, Division of Rare and Manuscript Collections, Cornell University, Ithaca, New York. Used by permission of the author's estate.

middle initial and last name—A., for *Aranea*, and *Cavatica*. Wilbur was the name of a pig actually owned by the Whites. The special setting created by White is revealed in the following quote:

> Life in the barn was very good—night and day winter and summer, spring and fall, dull days and bright days. It was the best place to be, thought Wilbur, this warm delicious cellar, with the garrulous geese, the changing seasons, the heat of the sun, the passage of swallows, the nearness of rats, the sameness of sheep, the love of spiders, the smell of manure, and the glory of everything.

The words of E. B. White, found in anthologies of great American essays, in the backpacks of college students, and in the eager hands of children of all ages, have touched, amused, and inspired millions of people. Readers of all ages continue to appreciate the lessons learned from Wilbur and his "true friend," Charlotte the spider who, like White, was also a "good writer."

FROM *Common Sense* AND *The American Crisis*

Thomas Paine

The sun never shined on a cause of greater worth. 'Tis not the affair of a city, a county, a province, or a kingdom; but of a continent—of at least one-eighth part of the habitable globe. 'Tis not the concern of a day, a year, or an age; posterity are virtually involved in the contest, and will be more or less affected even to the end of time, by the proceedings now. Now is the seed time of continental union, faith and honor.

These are the times that try men's souls. The summer soldier and the sunshine patriot will, in this crisis, shrink from the service of their country; but he that stands it now deserves the love and thanks of man and woman. Tyranny, like hell, is not easily conquered; yet we have this consolation with us, that the harder the conflict, the more glorious the triumph. What we obtain too cheap, we esteem too lightly—it is dearness only that gives everything its value. Heaven knows how to put a proper price upon its goods, and it would be strange indeed if so celestial an article as freedom should not be highly rated.

I turn with the warm ardor of a friend to those who have nobly stood, and are yet determined to stand the matter out. I call not upon a few, but upon all—not on this state or that state, but on every state—up and help us; lay your shoulders to the wheel. Better have too much force than too little, when so great an object is at stake.

Let it be told to the future world that in the depth of winter, when nothing but hope and virtue could survive, that the city and the country, alarmed at one common danger, came forth to meet and to repulse it. Say not that thousands are gone; turn out your tens of thousands. Throw not the burden of the day upon Providence, but "show your faith by your works," that God may bless you. It matters not where you live, or what rank of life you hold—the evil or the blessing will reach you all. The far and the near, the home countries and the back, the rich and poor will suffer or rejoice alike.

The heart that feels not now is dead; the blood of his children will curse his cowardice who shrinks back at a time when a little might have saved the whole, and made them happy. I love the man that can smile in trouble, that can gather strength from distress, and grow brave by reflection. 'Tis the business of little minds to shrink; but he whose heart is firm and whose conscience approves his conduct will pursue his principles unto death.

> I LOVE THE MAN THAT CAN SMILE IN TROUBLE, THAT CAN GATHER STRENGTH FROM DISTRESS, AND GROW BRAVE BY REFLECTION.

The American flag is displayed in the woods at Washington Island, Door County, Wisconsin. Photograph by Darryl R. Beers.

COLUMBIA'S FAVORITE SON

from THE PENNSYLVANIA GAZETTE, *November 4, 1789*

Great Washington, the hero's come;
Each heart exulting hears the sound.
Thousands to their deliverer throng
And shout him welcome all around!
　　Now in full chorus, join the song,
　　And shout aloud, "Great Washington!"

Then view Columbia's favorite son,
Her father, savior, friend, and guide.
There see the immortal Washington,
His country's glory, boast, and pride.
　　Now in full chorus, join the song,
　　And shout aloud, "Great Washington!"

When the impending storm of war,
Thick clouds, and darkness hid our way,
Great Washington, our polar star,
Arose; and all was light as day.
　　Now in full chorus, join the song,
　　And shout aloud, "Great Washington!"

'Twas on yon plains thy valor rose
And ran like fire from man to man;
'Twas here thou humbled Paria's foes,
And chased whole legions to the main.
　　Now in full chorus, join the song,
　　And shout aloud, "Great Washington!"

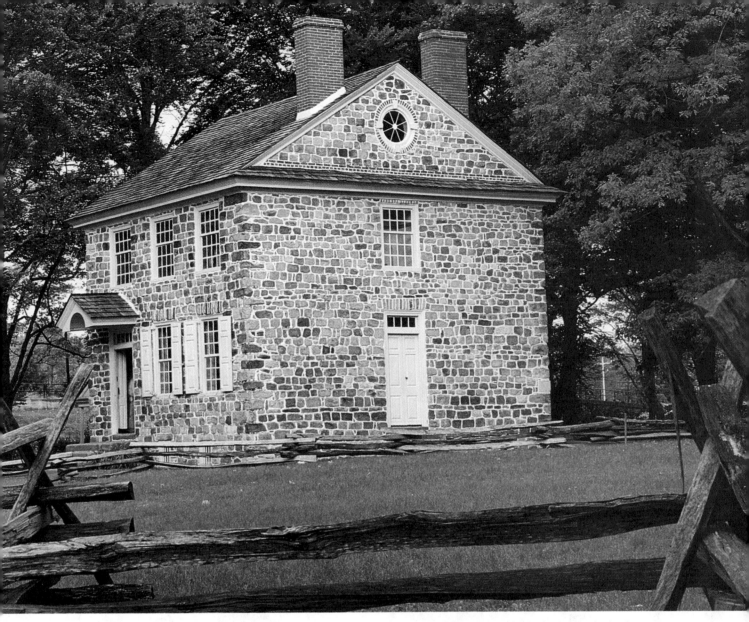

The Isaac Potts House was rented by General George Washington during the winter of 1777–78 in order to establish a headquarters for the coordination of the daily activities of the entire Continental Army at Valley Forge, Pennsylvania. Photograph by J. Blank/H. Armstrong Roberts.

Through countless dangers, toil, and cares,
Our hero led us safely on—
With matchless skill directs the wars,
Till Victory cries "The day's his own!"
    Now in full chorus, join the song,
    And shout aloud, "Great Washington!"

His country saved, the contest o'er,
Sweet peace restored, his toils to crown,
The warrior to his native shore
Returns and tills his fertile ground.
    Now in full chorus, join the song,
    And shout aloud, "Great Washington!"

But soon Columbia called him forth
Again to save her sinking fame;
To take the helm and by his worth
To make her an immortal name.
    Now in full chorus, join the song,
    And shout aloud, "Great Washington!"

Not yet alone through Paria's shores
Has fame her mighty trumpet blown;
E'en Europe, Africa, Asia, hear
And emulate the deeds he's done.
    Now in full chorus, join the song,
    And shout aloud, "Great Washington!"

Farewell Address to the People of the United States

George Washington, September 17, 1796

With slight shades of difference you have the same religion, manners, habits, and political principles. You have in a common cause fought and triumphed together. The independence and liberty you possess are the work of joint councils and joint efforts, of common dangers, sufferings, and successes.

This Government, the offspring of our own choice, uninfluenced and unawed, adopted upon full investigation and mature deliberation, completely free in its principles, in the distribution of its powers, uniting security with energy, and containing within itself a provision for its own amendment, has a just claim to your confidence and your support. Respect for its authority, compliance with its laws, acquiescence in its measures, are duties enjoined by the fundamental maxims of true liberty.

Liberty itself will find in such a government, with powers properly distributed and adjusted, its surest guardian.

Relying on its kindness, in this as in other things, and actuated by that fervent love towards it which is so natural to a man who views in it the native soil of himself and his progenitors for several generations, I anticipate with pleasing expectation that retreat, in which I promise myself to realize without alloy the sweet enjoyment of partaking in the midst of my fellow citizens the benign influence of good laws under a free government, the ever-favorite object of my heart, and the happy reward, as I trust, of our mutual cares, labors, and dangers.

WHEN THE FLAG GOES BY

Nancy Byrd Turner

Boy, bare your head when the flag goes by!
Girl, look to your loyalty as it waves!
Those stars came out in a splendid sky
Over your forefathers' gallant graves;
Those stripes were fastened by heroes' hands;

Those colors flash to the farthest lands.
A bit of bunting, but how it gleams,
Fashioned of valor and woven of dreams.
The wind's in its folds, they are floating high:
Oh, lift your hearts as the flag goes by!

INDEPENDENCE DAY

Inga Gilson Caldwell

Our country's birth! Raise high the flag that flies
Today, as always, symbol of sacrifice,
For freedom is not won by selfish men.
Raise high the flag, be proud remembering
Our country's struggles, how it met each test
Whenever danger threatened; our bequest
A princely dowry from a workman's wage—
God, make us worthy of our heritage.

The Flag Is Passing By

Henry Holcomb Bennett

Hats off!
Along the street there comes
A blare of bugles, a ruffle of drums,
A flash of color beneath the sky:
Hats off!
The flag is passing by!

Blue and crimson and white it shines,
Over the steel-tipped, ordered lines.
Hats off!
The colors before us fly;
But more than the flag is passing by.

Sea-fights and land-fights, grim and great,
Fought to make and to save the State:
Weary marches and sinking ships;
Cheers of victory on dying lips;

Days of plenty and years of peace;
March of a strong land's swift increase;
Equal justice, right and law,
Stately honor and reverend awe;

Sign of a nation, great and strong
To ward her people from foreign wrong.
Pride and glory and honor—all
Live in the colors to stand or fall.

Hats off!
Along the street there comes
A blare of bugles, a ruffle of drums;
And loyal hearts are beating high:
Hats off!
The flag is passing by!

The Anthem of America

Craig E. Sathoff

The anthem of America
Is found within its schools,
Where care is given for the child,
Not just for sets of rules.

The anthem of America
Is church bells ringing clear,
Inviting one and all to come
When church time draws near.

The anthem of America
Is friendly, smiling faces,
And holidays to celebrate,
And picnics, sports, and races.

It is clothing stores with ample choice
And hospitals for special care,
And harvests in abundant lots,
And carnivals and fairs.

It is people with the right to move
About their cherished land,
To visit freely where they wish,
To act as they have planned.

The anthem of America
Gives everyone the choice
To sing the part each chooses,
According to each voice.

Flag Day

Editorial from the NEW YORK TIMES, *June 14, 1940*

What's a flag? What's the love of country for which it stands? Maybe it begins with love of the land itself. It is the fog rolling in with the tide at Eastport, or through the Golden Gate and among the towers of San Francisco. It is the sun coming up behind the White Mountains, over the Green, throwing a shining glory on Lake Champlain and above the Adirondacks. It is the storied Mississippi rolling swift and muddy past St. Louis, rolling past Cairo, pouring down past the levees of New Orleans. It is lazy noontide in the pines of Carolina, it is a sea of wheat rippling in Western Kansas, it is the San Francisco peaks far north across the glowing nakedness of Arizona, it is the Grand Canyon and a little stream coming down out of a New England ridge, in which are trout.

It is men at work. It is the storm-tossed fishermen coming into Gloucester and Provincetown and Astoria. It is the farmer riding his great machine in the dust of harvest, the dairyman going to the barn before sunrise, the lineman mending the broken wire, the miner drilling for the blast. It is the teacher, doctor, and parson tending and helping, body and soul, for small reward.

It is small things remembered, the little corners of the land, the houses, the people that each one loves. We love our country because there was a little tree on a hill, and grass thereon, and a sweet valley below; because the hurdy-gurdy man came along on a sunny morning in a city street; because a beach or a farm or a lane or a house that might not seem much to others was once, for each of us, made magic. It is voices that are remembered only, no longer heard. It is parents, friends, the lazy chat of street and store and office, and the ease of mind that makes life tranquil. It is summer and winter, rain and sun and storms.

It is stories told. It is the Pilgrims dying in their first dreadful winter. It is the minuteman standing his ground at Concord Bridge, and dying there. It is the army in rags, sick, freezing, starving at Valley Forge. It is the wagons and the men on foot going westward over Cumberland Gap, floating down the great rivers, rolling over the great plains. It is the settler hacking fiercely at the primeval forest on his new, his own lands. It is Thoreau at Walden Pond, Lincoln at Cooper Union, and Lee riding home from Appomattox. It is corruption and disgrace, answered always by men who would not let the flag lie in the dust, who have stood up in every generation to fight for the old ideals and the old rights, at risk of ruin or of life itself.

It is a great multitude of people on pilgrimage, common and ordinary people, charged with the usual human failings, yet filled with such a hope as never caught the imaginations and the hearts of any nation on earth before. The hope of liberty. The hope of justice. The hope of a land in which a man can stand straight, without fear, without rancor.

The land and the people and the flag—the land a continent, the people of every race, the flag a symbol of what humanity may aspire to when the wars are over and the barriers are down; to these each generation must be dedicated and consecrated anew, to defend with life itself, if need be, but, above all, in friendliness, in hope, in courage, to live for.

A sailboat stands ready in Heritage Harbor, Grand Traverse Bay, Lake Michigan. Photograph by Darryl R. Beers.

READERS' FORUM

Snapshots from our IDEALS readers

Left: Helen Olsen, of East Troy, Wisconsin, sent this picture of her granddaughter Andrea holding a bag of cherry tomatoes and gladiolas, which she helped plant.

Below Left: Maggie Elizabeth Williams is carefully picking flowers out of "Grandbud" and Grandma's yard in Wilson, North Carolina. She is the granddaughter of Jack and Linda Williams.

Below Right: William "Will" Marshall Andrews III, two years old, is perfectly content to swing the day away while enjoying a vacation at the Outer Banks in North Carolina with his grandparents, Bill and Charlotte Andrews of Hopewell, Virginia.

Above: Jennifer Marie
Trout generously shares her
apple with the neighborhood's favorite pet. She is the three-
year-old granddaughter of Dee J. McDaniel of Scottsbluff,
Nebraska.

Right: A cool tower—Maria, Luissa, and Trevor Tallo enjoy a hot
summer day. They are the grandchildren of
Janet Mills of Rush, New York.

Below Right: Grandma Susan Poyner of Fort Branch, Indiana,
sends this photo of nineteen-month-old Maxwell Spencer Jackson
of Avon. He enjoyed this tractor at the Hendricks County
Fair so much that he did not want to do anything else.

THANK YOU for sharing your family photographs with *Ideals*. We hope to hear from
other readers who would like to share snapshots with the *Ideals* family. Please include a
self-addressed, stamped envelope if you
would like the photos returned. Keep your
original photographs for safekeeping and
send duplicate photos along with your
name, address, and telephone number to:

Readers' Forum
Ideals Publications
535 Metroplex Drive, Suite 250
Nashville, Tennessee 37211

ideals

Publisher, Patricia A. Pingry
Editor, Marjorie Lloyd
Designer, Marisa Calvin
Copy Editor, Melinda Rathjen
Permissions Editor, Patsy Jay
Contributing Writers, Lansing Christman,
Maud Dawson, Lois Winston, Pamela Kennedy,
D. Fran Morley, and Melinda Rathjen

ACKNOWLEDGMENTS

THE NEW YORK TIMES. "New York Times Editorial, June 14, 1940." Copyright © 1940 by The New York Times Company. Used by permission. SCARBROUGH, GEORGE. "Tenantry." Used by permission of the author. TABER, GLADYS. An excerpt from *Another Path.* Copyright © 1963 by Gladys Taber, renewed © 1991 by Constance Taber Colby. J. B. Lippincot Co., publisher. Reprinted by permission of Brandt & Hochman Literary Agents. Our thanks to the the Estate of Inga Gilson Caldwell, the Estate of Reginald Holmes, the Estate of Dan A. Hoover, the Estate of Edna Jaques, the Estate of Adeline Roseberg, the Estate of Craig E. Sathoff, the Estate of Samuel Harden Stille, and the Estate of Nancy Byrd Turner for permission to use the authors' material. Our sincere thanks to all those authors, some of whom we were unable to locate, who submitted material for publication.

Above: "Angel in a bucket"—that is how Vicki Morgan describes her youngest grandchild, three-year-old Emily Rose Hall, who lives only one block away in Volga, South Dakota.

Below Right: Let's go! One-year-old Lauren is ready to roll in her new red wagon. She is the daughter of Chuck and Tammy Huffman of Cleveland, Virginia.

Introducing . . .
THE IDEALS TREASURY OF FAITH IN AMERICA

God moves through America's history...trace His movements and claim your rich spiritual heritage. Discover rock-solid certainty that He is with you today.

The Ideals Treasury of Faith in America shows you where to look for God's hand. This inspiring new book presents dozens of eyewitness accounts to the greatest moments in our nation's history. These vibrant, faith-filled writings—from America's leaders, as well as ordinary citizens—will move and exhilarate you.

YOUR FREE GIFT

Full color photographs and paintings of American landmarks, events and sights accompany each written piece. Plus, patriotic songs, poems heralding liberty, and prayers for God's direction embellish this indispensable American treasury, making it as much of a pleasure to browse through as to read.

Exclusive highlights . . .
- ★ 160 Pages, heavy-weight enamel.
- ★ Reproductions of masterful paintings & historical documents.
- ★ Full-color photographs of America's landmarks.

Complete the Free Examination Certificate and mail today for your 21-Day Preview.

You will receive a FREE *Prayers for America* booklet just for ordering.

No need to send money now!

A compelling new book celebrating the spiritual journeys of an American astronaut and his wife . . .

High Calling

Experience God's love as He guides a family through a spiritual awakening.

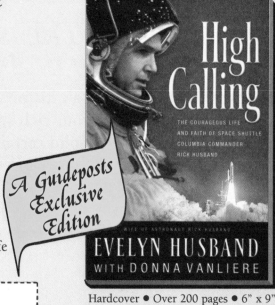

A Guideposts Exclusive Edition

Hardcover • Over 200 pages • 6" x 9"

High Calling is written by Evelyn Husband, wife of the late Rick Husband, Commander of the Space Shuttle Columbia.

High Calling is a beautifully written chronicle of a man who followed his heart and realized his life's dream with the help of a loving God. It is also the uplifting story of a devoted and caring wife who played a vital role in his life and helped him achieve success.

High Calling accounts the personal journeys of two people who loved each other and their spiritual journeys as they put God first in their lives.

This edition of *High Calling* featuring a personal introduction by Evelyn Husband is a Guideposts Exclusive. It is not sold in stores. To own this uplifting and faith-building book, return your 30-day Free Examination Certificate today.

Save OVER 30% OFF Publisher's Price!

Only $16.96

payable in 2 installments of $8.48 each, plus shipping and processing.

No need to send money now!

FREE EXAMINATION CERTIFICATE

YES! I'd like to examine *High Calling* at no risk or obligation. If I decide to keep the book, I will be billed later at the low Guideposts price of only $16.96, payable in 2 installments of $8.48 each, plus shipping and processing. If not completely satisfied, I may return the book within 30 days and owe nothing. The FREE 3-piece Personal Inspirational Set is mine to keep no matter what I decide.

Total copies ordered: _____

Please print your name and address:

_____
NAME

_____
ADDRESS   APT#

_____
CITY   STATE   ZIP

Allow 4 weeks for delivery. Orders subject to credit approval.
Send no money now. We will bill you later.
www.guidepostsbooks.com

Printed in USA
11/202209591

FREE GIFT FOR YOU!
Just for saying "yes," you will receive a 3-piece Personal Inspiration Set! Includes a Bookmark, Key Tag and Prayer Card featuring Rick Husband's favorite Bible verse from Proverbs 3:5-6.